HOW TO GET
what you *really* want

NORTH POINT
RESOURCES

HOW TO GET WHAT YOU REALLY WANT

Study Guide

LEADER INFO **4**

HOW TO USE THIS STUDY **5**

PART 1 .... **6**

PART 2 .... **12**

PART 3 .... **18**

PART 4 .... **24**

Here are some ideas to get you started.

LEADERS:

Need some help? It's okay. We all do.

A full walk-through of the study guide with notes on how to navigate each session is available at **groupleaders.org/reallywant.**

VIDEOS:

The video sessions that complement this study can be found on the:

- **Anthology Mobile App** (free on the Apple App Store and Google Play)

- *How to Get What You Really Want* DVD (available on Amazon)

POST A
PICTURE OF
YOUR GROUP USING
#reallywant

Your next study could be on us!

1. HANG OUT.

(about 30 minutes)

Our lives move so fast these days. Take some time to talk about what's going on in the lives of those in your group. Asking about things like job interviews, the health of their kids, and how their weeks are going goes a long way in building community.

2. WATCH THE VIDEO AND DOODLE ALONG.

(about 20 minutes)

When we designed this study guide, we had note-taking in mind. So while you're watching the video, take advantage of the extra space and grid pages for notes and/or drawings, depending on your note-taking style.

3. DISCUSS AND COMPLETE THE ACTIVITIES.

(about 45 minutes)

Depending on the session, your group will have Discussion Questions and scenarios to think through, as well as activities to do. Putting pen to paper can give you deeper insight into the content.

4. PRAY.

(about 5 minutes)

Keep it simple and real. Use the prayer provided. Ask God to help you apply what you've learned that week.

PART 1

Careful What You Want For

VIDEO RECAP

What do you **want?**

We want our _____.

- When we **get** our way, we often **get** in our own way.

We want to do what we want to do.

We want perpetual _____.

- Pleasure is addictive, which undermines the pleasure, which **isn't** what we want.

We want it _____!

- Later is **longer**.
- Regret **begins** with "I want."
- Regret ends with "I **want** to go back in time and **not get** what I **wanted**."

If we always **get** our way, we _____ our way.

If we always do what we **want to do**, we end up where we **don't want to be**.

If we get what we want **now**, we may not get what we want _____.

> What **causes** fights and quarrels among you? Don't **they** come from your desires that **battle** within you? You _____ but do not **have**, so you **kill**. You **covet** but you cannot get what you **want**, so you quarrel and fight...
>
> (James 4:1-2 NIV)

What we **really want** lurks in a realm we **rarely explore**.

POST A PICTURE OF YOUR GROUP USING **#reallywant**

Your next study could be on us!

Answer Key for Blanks

way	NOW	later
pleasure	lose	desire

LET'S TALK ABOUT IT

1 Andy joked about being grateful for "unanswered prayers." What are some things you wanted at one time (perhaps when you were younger) but are now grateful you didn't get?

2 Have you or someone you know ever had a seemingly innocent want become a pathway to a sin, habit, or regret?

3 Take a few minutes to write down examples of when you experienced these downsides of getting what you wanted. If you'd like, share one of your examples with the group.

- I wanted my own way...*but I ended up getting in the way.*

- I wanted to do what I wanted to do...*but it got me where I didn't want to be.*

- I wanted perpetual pleasure...*but it eventually stopped being pleasurable.*

- I wanted it now...*but I didn't want it later.*

4 In the message, Andy said, "Most of us don't know what we *really* want because we're so distracted by our desires and appetites…what we can have now." Can you identify anything you currently want that has the potential to distract you from what you ultimately, *really* want?

Notes

THIS WEEK, THINK ABOUT...

James 4:1 says, "What causes fights and quarrels among you? Don't they come from your desires that battle within you?"

When a disagreement arises for you this week, stop and say (maybe out loud):

Do you know what the problem is? I'm not getting what I want.

We've all seen *wants* eventually kill opportunities, careers, and even marriages. If we don't understand what's behind our wants—what's going on in our hearts—we have the potential to destroy the things and relationships that matter most in our lives.

PRAYER

God, I want to understand the heart behind my wants. Help me see which desires have the potential to distract me from what matters most in my life.

IF WE *always* DO WHAT WE WANT TO DO, WE END UP *where we* DON'T WANT TO BE. TO BE.

POST A
PICTURE OF
YOUR GROUP USING
#reallywant

Your next study could be on us!

PART 2

Don't Be Deceived

VIDEO RECAP

Choosing _____ is _____.

> *I **do not** understand what I **do**. For what I **want** to do I do not do, but what I **hate** I **do**. And if I do what I do not **want** to do, I agree that the **law** is good… For I have the **desire** to do what is good, but I **cannot** carry it out. For I do not do the good I **want** to do, but the evil I do not **want** to do—this I keep on doing.*
>
> (Romans 7:15–16, 18–19 NIV)

What we **naturally** want is often in conflict with what we _____ want.

Human **Nature**

- Cheating
- Lying
- Racism
- Adultery
- Me First
- Revenge

When you follow the desires of your sinful **nature**, *the results are* _____ _____:
sexual immorality, impurity, lustful pleasures, idolatry, sorcery, hostility, quarreling, **jealousy**, *outbursts of anger,* **selfish** *ambition, dissension, division, envy,* **drunkenness**...

(Galatians 5:19–21 NLT)

...but each person is tempted when they are _____ _____ *by their own evil desire and enticed. Then, after* **desire** *has conceived, it gives birth to* **sin**; *and sin, when it is full-grown, gives birth to* **death**. *Don't be* _____, *my dear brothers and sisters.*

(James 1:14–16 NIV)

POST A PICTURE OF YOUR GROUP USING #reallywant

Your next study could be on us!

Answer Key for Blanks

valuable	ultimately	dragged away
unnatural	very clear	deceived

(Notes)

LET'S TALK ABOUT IT

1 What is a change you have tried to make through personal discipline or willpower? How long did the change last?

2 Look at the description of sinful nature in Galatians 5:19–21. How does this match or conflict with your personal outlook on humanity?

When you follow the desires of your sinful nature, the results are very clear: sexual immorality, impurity, lustful pleasures, idolatry, sorcery, hostility, quarreling, jealousy, outbursts of anger, selfish ambition, dissension, division, envy, drunkenness...

3 In the message, Andy urged, "Don't trade *ultimate* for *immediate*."

- Talk about a time you've seen someone make the choice to prioritize long-term goals over short-term desire or pleasure.

- What is one area of life in which you have trouble making the same choice?

4 James 1:14 says, "*...but each person is tempted when they are dragged away by their own evil desire and enticed.*" Using the chart below, identify what has dragged you away (or has the potential to drag you away) from the things you ultimately want. If you're comfortable doing so, share one of your answers with the group.

WHAT I ULTIMATELY WANT	WHAT DRAGGED ME AWAY
Financial health	*Trying to keep up with others*

Notes

THIS WEEK, THINK ABOUT...

Chasing what you want *now* has the potential to kill your dreams, opportunities, and relationships. It can put what you *really* want out of reach.

1. What do you really want?

2. What's dragging you away?

3. How long do you plan to let what you naturally want drag you away from what you ultimately want?

PRAYER

God, help me break my unhealthy appetites. Help me discover and pursue what I really value over what I want.

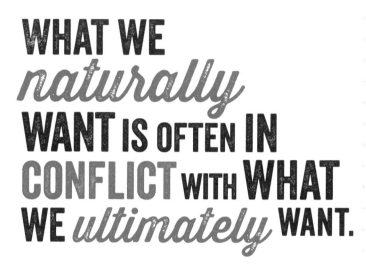

WHAT WE *naturally* WANT IS OFTEN IN CONFLICT WITH WHAT WE *ultimately* WANT.

POST A PICTURE OF YOUR GROUP USING #reallywant

Your next study could be on us!

PART 3
Last Things First

VIDEO RECAP

"If you carefully consider what you
_____ to be said of you in the
funeral experience, you will find **your** definition
of _____."

—Steven Covey

Sin became synonymous with **failure**.

To get what you really want, you must
_____ what you **really** value.

What does God **really** want?

What does God **really** want _____ us?

*But the **fruit** of the Spirit is love, joy, peace,
patience, kindness, goodness, faithfulness,
gentleness, self-control...*

(Galatians 5:22–23 NASB)

*Since we live by the Spirit, let us **keep in step** with the Spirit. Let us not become conceited, **provoking** and envying each other.*

(Galatians 5:25–26 NIV)

POST A PICTURE OF YOUR GROUP USING
#reallywant

Your next study could be on us!

Answer Key for Blanks

wanted	discover
success	for

LET'S TALK ABOUT IT

1 Take a few minutes and begin the process of thinking through the funeral exercise Andy mentions. Select some of the words below that reflect what you would want people to say about you.

Accepting	Accountable	Achieving	Adventurous
Ambitious	Attractive	Balanced	Bold
Brilliant	Calm	Caring	Charitable
Cheerful	Clever	Committed	Compassionate
Consistent	Creative	Credible	Daring
Decisive	Dedicated	Dependable	Empathetic
Encouraging	Enthusiastic	Ethical	Fair
Family Oriented	Generous	Goal Oriented	Grateful
Happy	Healthy	Honest	Humble
Humorous	Independent	Innovative	Inspiring
Intelligent	Joyful	Kind	A Leader
Loving	Loyal	Admired	Motivated
Optimistic	Passionate	Professional	Spiritual
Perfect	Popular	Powerful	Respected
Reliable	Resilient	Resourceful	Selfless
Successful	Thankful	Thoughtful	Trustworthy

Notes

2 Andy said that doing the funeral exercise helped him realize his definition of success had nothing to do with his accomplishments and everything to do with his character. What do the words you selected reveal about how *you* define success?

3 What are two things you're currently doing to pursue your definition of success (i.e., to exhibit the words you chose in the funeral exercise)?

4 Is there anything you're currently putting energy toward that doesn't align with your definition of success?

5 *But the fruit of the Spirit is love, joy, peace, patience, kindness, goodness, faithfulness, gentleness, self-control...*
                              (Galatians 5:22–23 NASB)

- Is there a fruit of the Spirit you worry might interfere with your personal or professional goals?
- Are there parallels between the list of fruits of the Spirit and the words you chose in the funeral exercise?

Notes

THIS WEEK, THINK ABOUT...

Consider reading *The 7 Habits of Highly Effective People* by Stephen Covey. Think through what you would want a family member, a close friend, and a colleague/peer to say about you in a eulogy.

What can you begin doing this week to cultivate the qualities you really value?

PRAYER

God, it's encouraging to see that what I ultimately want is, in fact, aligned with what you want for me. Help me pursue a definition of success that brings you glory and leads me to a life of purpose.

To get WHAT YOU REALLY WANT, you MUST DISCOVER WHAT YOU really VALUE.

POST A
PICTURE OF
YOUR GROUP USING
#reallywant

Your next study could be on us!

PART 4
Thinkin' It Through

VIDEO RECAP

*Therefore, I **urge** you, brothers and sisters, in view of God's _____, to offer your **bodies** as a living _____, holy and pleasing to God—this is your **true** and **proper** worship. Do not **conform** to the pattern of this world, but be **transformed by** the **renewing** of your **mind**...*

(Romans 12:1–2 NIV)

When we see as God sees, we are more inclined to do as God says.

New Testament **imperatives**
apart from
New Testament **thinking**
result in
short-term **obedience**
and
long-term **frustration**.

*...Then you will be able to **test** and **approve**
what **God's will** is—his _____,
_____ and _____ will.*

(Romans 12:2 NIV)

POST A
PICTURE OF
YOUR GROUP USING
#reallywant

Your next study could be on us!

Answer Key for Blanks

mercy   good   perfect

sacrifice   pleasing

Notes

LET'S TALK ABOUT IT

1 Can you share any examples of having *"conform[ed] to the pattern of this world"*? (Hint: What did you get or upgrade just to keep up with everyone else?)

2 The apostle Paul suggested that transformation begins by renewing your mind (instead of beginning by changing your behavior).

- If you grew up in church, how does this match or conflict with what you learned?

- What are some practical ways to renew your mind—or, as Andy said, to "learn to see as God sees"?

3 Andy shared the word picture that renewing your mind is like refinishing furniture. *"You have to take off the old and put on the new."*

• Take a few minutes to complete the chart below.

I WANT TO SEE MY _____ AS GOD SEES IT.	WHAT I NATURALLY WANT... ("Take off the old.")	WHAT I ULTIMATELY WANT... ("Put on the new.")
Career	The corner office	The respect of my adult kids

• Does this framework reveal any changes you need to make to pursue what you *ultimately* want?

Notes

THIS WEEK, THINK ABOUT...

When you discover what you really value—what you really want—don't be surprised if you come face to face with the will of your heavenly Father.

What are you doing now that's going to undermine what you ultimately want?

PRAYER

God, I want to see as you see. I want to pursue what ultimately matters, not conform to the pattern of this world. Transform my mind so I can better know your will and give me the courage to follow it.

WHEN WE SEE *as God sees,* WE ARE MORE INCLINED *to do* AS GOD SAYS.

POST A PICTURE OF YOUR GROUP USING #reallywant

Your next study could be on us!

Notes

Notes